Represent and Solve Problems Involving Division

Wendy Young

New York

Published in 2015 by The Rosen Publishing Group, Inc.
29 East 21st Street, New York, NY 10010

Book Design: Jonathan J. D'Rozario

Photo Credits: Cover YanLev/Shutterstock.com; pp. 3, 7, 9, 11, 13, 15, 17, 23 (paper) Seregam/Shutterstock.com; pp. 3, 4, 6, 7, 8, 9, 10, 11, 12, 13, 14, 15, 16, 18, 20, 21, 22, 23, 24 (wood) CoffeeChocolates/Shutterstock.com; pp. 4, 6, 8, 10, 12, 14, 16, 18, 20, 22, 24 (cutting board) turtix/Shutterstock.com; pp. 5, 22 spotmatik/Shutterstock.com; p. 7 (oatmeal) Timolina/Shutterstock.com; p. 7 (milk) Vladimir V. Georgievskiy/Shutterstock.com; p. 9 (eggs) Aleksandrs Samuilovs/Shutterstock.com; p. 9 (main) MSPhotographic/Shutterstock.com; p. 11 (sandwich) Nitr/Shutterstock.com; p. 11 (bread) nito/Shutterstock.com; p. 13 (quesadilla) Brent Hofacker/Shutterstock.com; p. 13 (bean) lobster20/Shutterstock.com; p. 15 (broccoli) Kalin Eftimov/Shutterstock.com; p. 15 (broccoli bowl) Oliver Hoffmann/Shutterstock.com; p. 17 (pepper) Aaron Amat/Shutterstock.com; p. 17 (pizza) Vitality Netiaga/Shutterstock.com; p. 19 John S. Quinn/Shutterstock.com; p. 21 Photographee.eu/Shutterstock.com.

ISBN: 978-1-4777-4713-1
6-pack ISBN: 978-1-4777-4711-7
Manufactured in the United States of America

CPSIA Compliance Information: Batch #WS15RC: For further information contact Rosen Publishing, New York, New York at 1-800-237-9932.

Contents

Make Your Own Meals

Do you know how to make your own food? Cooking can be a fun hobby, and it can be good for you, too!

What kinds of meals would you like to make? Most people eat 3 meals a day: breakfast, lunch, and dinner. You can also learn how to make snacks. You don't have to be a chef to make a good meal. There are plenty of **recipes** for beginners!

When you make meals, you should include **ingredients** from the 5 food groups, which are vegetables, fruits, protein foods, dairy, and grains.

Breakfast

It's important to eat breakfast every day. Many breakfasts are made of grains. The grain group includes cereal, oatmeal, and wheat bread.

Oatmeal helps keep you feeling full. To make oatmeal, you have to boil milk on the stove and add oats. Stir the oats until the milk is **absorbed**. Make sure an adult helps whenever you cook with the stove or oven. Add cinnamon or fruit, such as apples, for extra taste!

Imagine you need 8 cups of milk to make oatmeal for your family. If 1 quart has 4 cups, how many quarts will you need? You can divide to find out.

$8 \div 4 = 2$

Another great food group you need to start your day is protein. Protein foods include meat, beans, eggs, and nuts. They help your bones and muscles grow.

An omelet is a great breakfast protein food. It's eggs that are folded over fillings, such as cheese, vegetables, or meat. To make one, crack 2 eggs, mix them, and drop them in a frying pan. When the omelet seems solid, add yummy fillings and fold it over.

If there are 12 eggs in your egg carton, you can make 6 omelets that have 2 eggs each.

$$12 \div 6 = 2$$

What's for Lunch?

The most important part of making a meal healthy is making sure you have **variety**. That means you should try to include as many of the food groups as possible.

Making a sandwich for lunch is a great example of variety. For a healthy sandwich, you could use whole-wheat bread, turkey, lettuce, and tomatoes. On the side, have an apple and glass of milk. That lunch uses all 5 food groups!

If your loaf of bread is 24 centimeters long and there are 12 pieces altogether, each piece is 2 centimeters wide.

24 ÷ 12 = 2

24 cm
2 cm

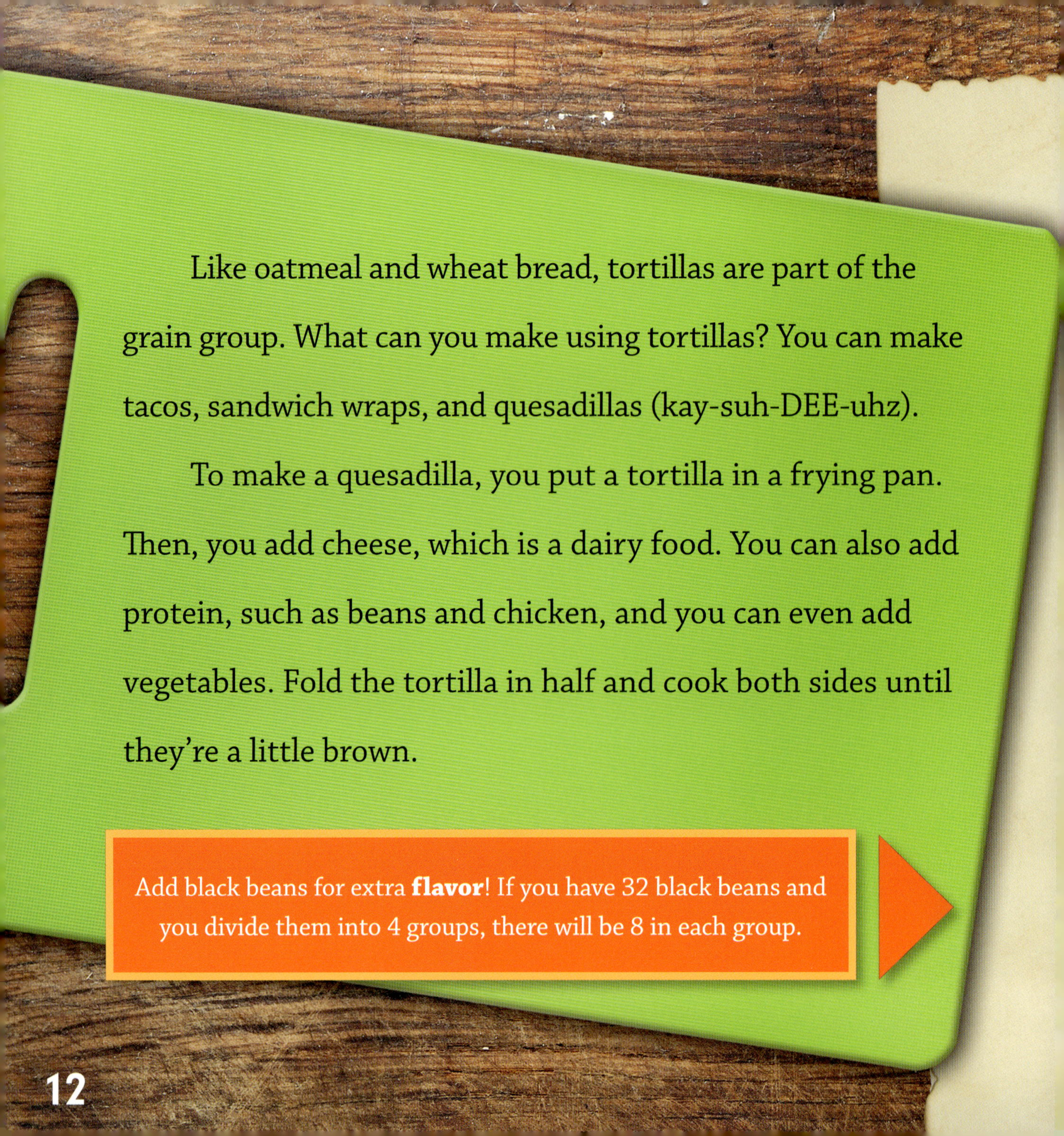

Like oatmeal and wheat bread, tortillas are part of the grain group. What can you make using tortillas? You can make tacos, sandwich wraps, and quesadillas (kay-suh-DEE-uhz).

To make a quesadilla, you put a tortilla in a frying pan. Then, you add cheese, which is a dairy food. You can also add protein, such as beans and chicken, and you can even add vegetables. Fold the tortilla in half and cook both sides until they're a little brown.

Add black beans for extra **flavor**! If you have 32 black beans and you divide them into 4 groups, there will be 8 in each group.

$$32 \div 4 = 8$$

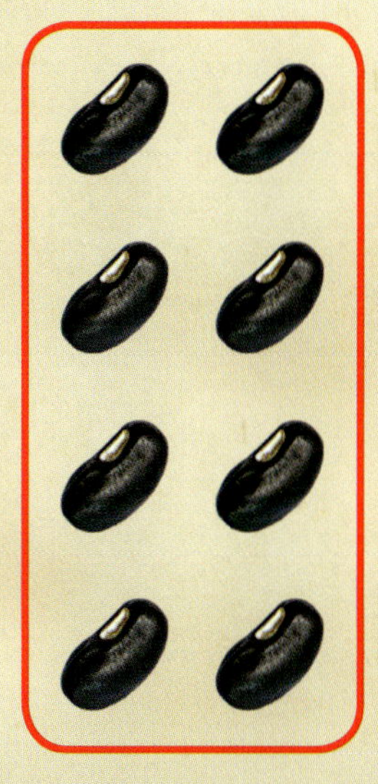   

Let's Eat Dinner!

Dinner is a great time to eat from all 5 food groups! **Nutritionists** say you should imagine your dinner plate is cut into 4 parts. The parts should hold a fruit, vegetable, protein food, and grain. Imagine a cup of dairy on the side, such as yogurt or a glass of milk.

An example of a healthy dinner would be broccoli, chicken, grapes, and a wheat roll, with milk on the side.

Broccoli is a very healthy vegetable! If you have 36 pieces of broccoli and you have 6 people in your family, how many pieces can each person eat at dinner? You can put 6 pieces of broccoli on each plate.

$$36 \div 6 = 6$$

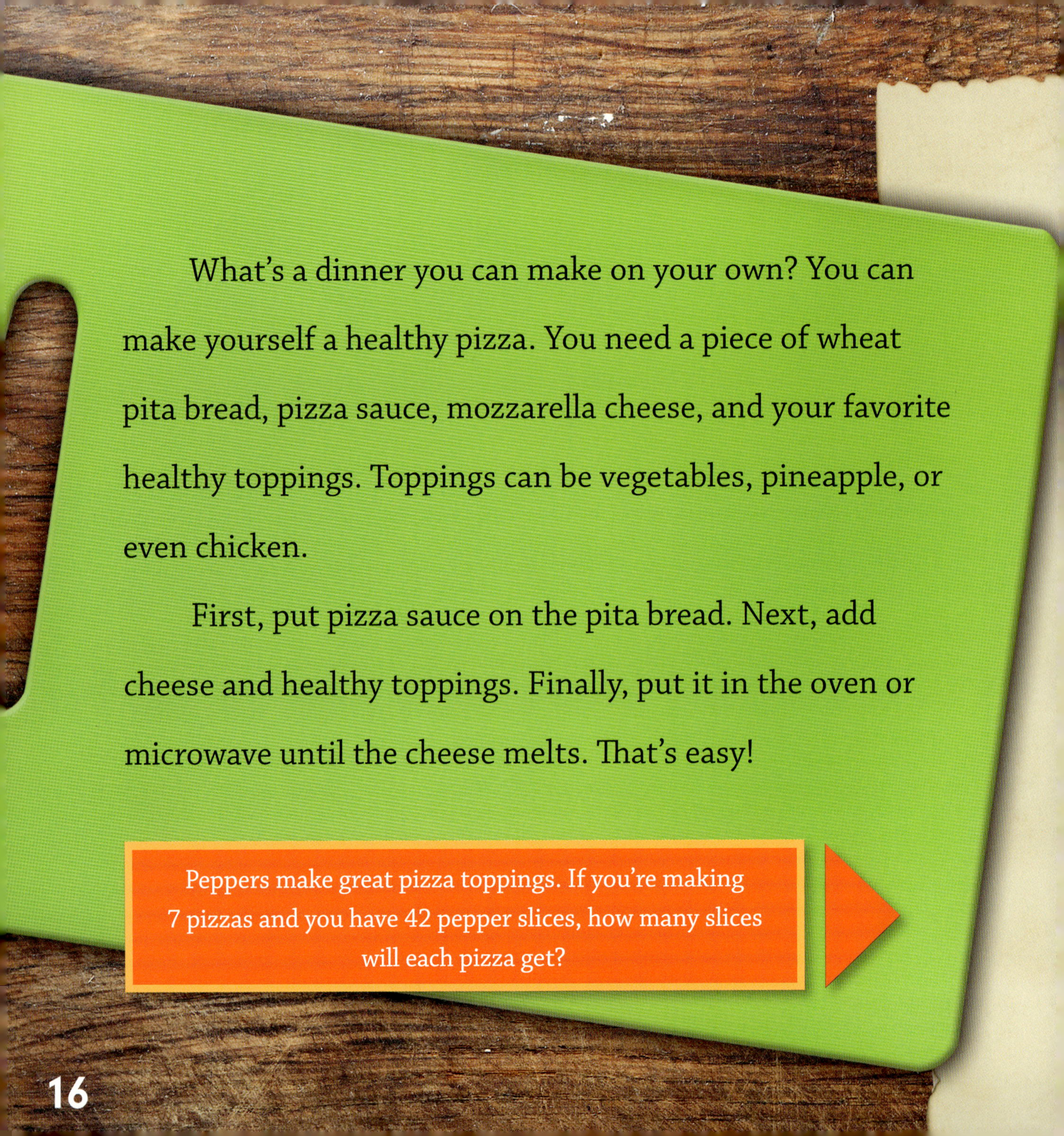

What's a dinner you can make on your own? You can make yourself a healthy pizza. You need a piece of wheat pita bread, pizza sauce, mozzarella cheese, and your favorite healthy toppings. Toppings can be vegetables, pineapple, or even chicken.

First, put pizza sauce on the pita bread. Next, add cheese and healthy toppings. Finally, put it in the oven or microwave until the cheese melts. That's easy!

Peppers make great pizza toppings. If you're making 7 pizzas and you have 42 pepper slices, how many slices will each pizza get?

42 ÷ 7 = ?

Snack Time

When you're hungry between meals, it's time for a healthy snack! Having a healthy snack can be as simple as eating a single fruit or vegetable.

Yogurt is a very healthy dairy snack. To make a berry yogurt parfait (pahr-FAY), put yogurt in a cup, about an inch high. Then, put berries on top, about an inch high. Add more yogurt, then more berries. You can put nuts or granola on top, too.

Blueberries taste great with yogurt! If you have 63 blueberries and you put them into 7 groups, how many berries are in each group?

$63 \div 7 = ?$

Fruits and vegetables can be easy to eat on their own. You can always pack a banana, an apple, or some carrots with you for a snack. But there are other ways to eat healthy snacks, too.

To make a fruit kebab (kuh-BAHB), you first need a skewer, which is a long, thin stick. Then, you stick fruit pieces, such as kiwi, strawberries, and bananas, on the skewer. You can put cheese on there, too!

You can get creative with your kebab! If you have 72 strawberry pieces and 9 friends, how many pieces will each friend get?

$$72 \div 9 = ?$$

Healthy Recipes

There are many different recipes you can use. Sometimes you'll need help from an adult. But some recipes are easy and safe enough for beginners.

The trick to making healthy meals is to include as many of the food groups as possible. Healthy meals give you energy to exercise and play! That helps your body stay strong. What's your favorite recipe?

absorb (uhb-ZOHRB) To take in or soak up.

flavor (FLAY-vuhr) How something tastes.

ingredient (ihn-GREE-dee-uhnt) Food used when cooking.

nutritionist (noo-TRIH-shuh-nihst) Someone who has studied which foods are healthy and why.

recipe (REH-suh-pee) A set of instructions for making food.

variety (vuh-RY-uh-tee) A number of different things.

Index